CW01217642

WIND AND WATER SHAPE THE LAND

By NADIA HIGGINS
Illustrations by JIA LIU
Music by ERIK KOSKINEN

CANTATA LEARNING

WWW.CANTATALEARNING.COM

CANTATA LEARNING

Published by Cantata Learning
1710 Roe Crest Drive
North Mankato, MN 56003
www.cantatalearning.com

Copyright © 2018 Cantata Learning

All rights reserved. No part of this publication may be reproduced
in any form without written permission from the publisher.

Library of Congress Cataloging-in-Publication Data
Names: Higgins, Nadia, author. | Liu, Jia (Illustrator), illustrator. |
  Koskinen, Erik, composer.
Title: Wind and water shape the land / by Nadia Higgins ; illustrated by Jia
  Liu ; music by Erik Koskinen.
Description: North Mankato, MN : Cantata Learning, [2018] | Series: What
  shapes our Earth? | Includes lyrics and sheet music. | Audience: Ages 6–9.
  | Audience: K to grade 3. | Includes bibliographical references.
Identifiers: LCCN 2017017516 (print) | LCCN 2017036114 (ebook) | ISBN
  9781684101764 (ebook) | ISBN 9781684101214 (hardcover : alk. paper)
Subjects: LCSH: Weathering--Juvenile literature. | Erosion--Juvenile
  literature. | Children's songs, English.
Classification: LCC QE570 (ebook) | LCC QE570 .H444 2018 (print) | DDC
  551.3/02--dc23
LC record available at https://lccn.loc.gov/2017017516

Book design and art direction, Tim Palin Creative
Editorial direction, Kellie M. Hultgren
Music direction, Elizabeth Draper
Music arranged and produced by Erik Koskinen

Printed in the United States of America in North Mankato, Minnesota.
122017   0378CGS18

ACCESS THE MUSIC!
SCAN CODE WITH MOBILE APP
CANTATALEARNING.COM

TIPS TO SUPPORT LITERACY AT HOME

WHY READING AND SINGING WITH YOUR CHILD IS SO IMPORTANT

Daily reading with your child leads to increased academic achievement. Music and songs, specifically rhyming songs, are a fun and easy way to build early literacy and language development. Music skills correlate significantly with both phonological awareness and reading development. Singing helps build vocabulary and speech development. And reading and appreciating music together is a wonderful way to strengthen your relationship.

READ AND SING EVERY DAY!

TIPS FOR USING CANTATA LEARNING BOOKS AND SONGS DURING YOUR DAILY STORY TIME

1. As you sing and read, point out the different words on the page that rhyme. Suggest other words that rhyme.

2. Memorize simple rhymes such as Itsy Bitsy Spider and sing them together. This encourages comprehension skills and early literacy skills.

3. Use the questions in the back of each book to guide your singing and storytelling.

4. Read the included sheet music with your child while you listen to the song. How do the music notes correlate to the words of the song?

5. Sing along on the go and at home. Access music by scanning the QR code on each Cantata book, or by using the included CD. You can also stream or download the music for free to your computer, smartphone, or mobile device.

Devoting time to daily reading shows that you are available for your child. Together, you are building language, literacy, and listening skills.

Have fun reading and singing!

Every day, the land around you is changing. The changes happen slowly. You may not notice. But wind and water are always at work. When wind blows and water flows, they shape the land. This is called **erosion**.

Turn the page. Sing along to this wet and windy song!

5

Blowing wind and flowing water wear down rock and carry sand.

Two of Earth's most powerful forces, wind and water shape the land.

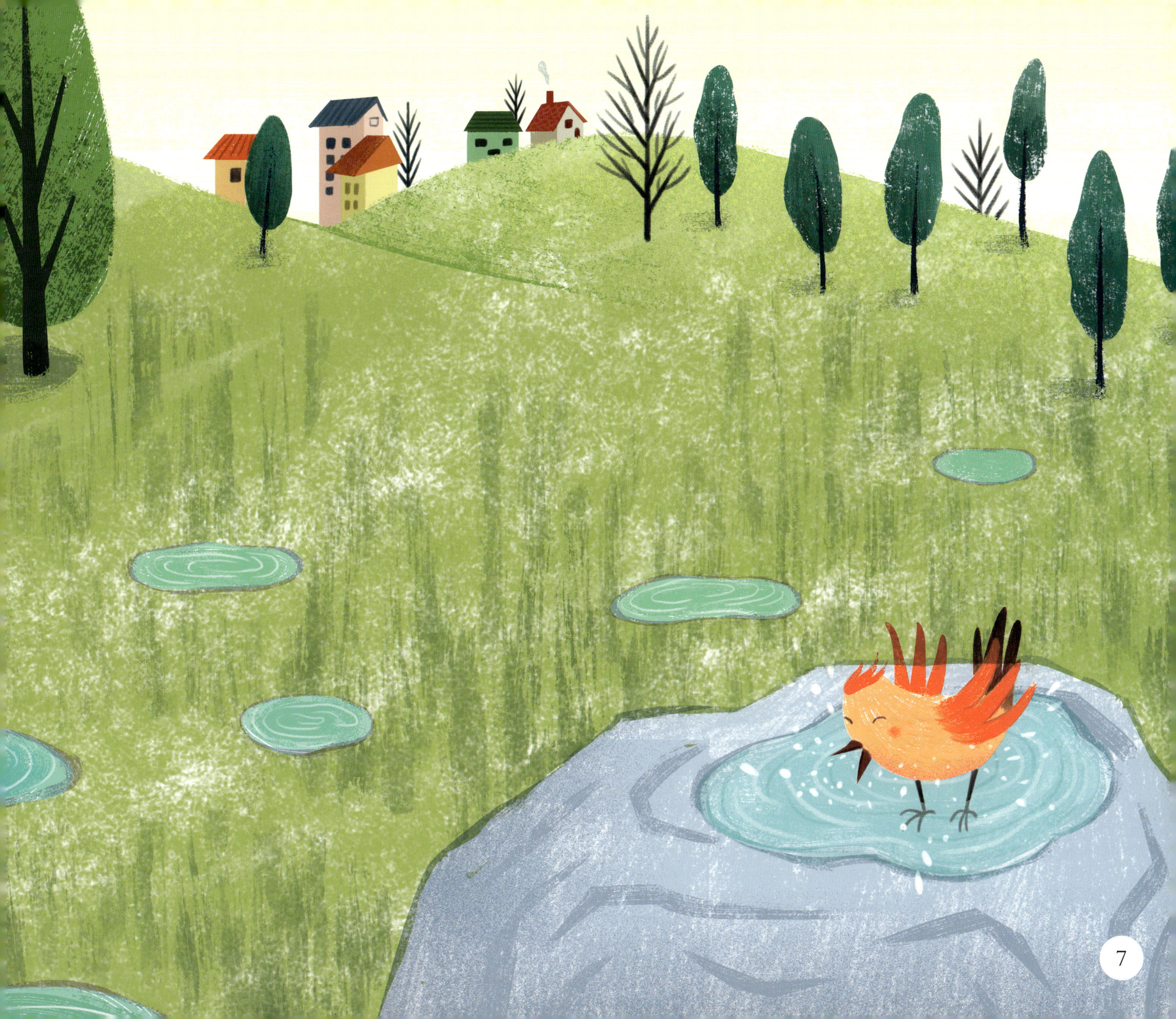

With one wave, two, a million more
the ocean water pounds the shore.

Crashing waves and sprays of mist
chip away at towering cliffs.

9

Blowing wind and flowing water wear down rock and carry sand.

Two of Earth's most powerful forces, wind and water shape the land.

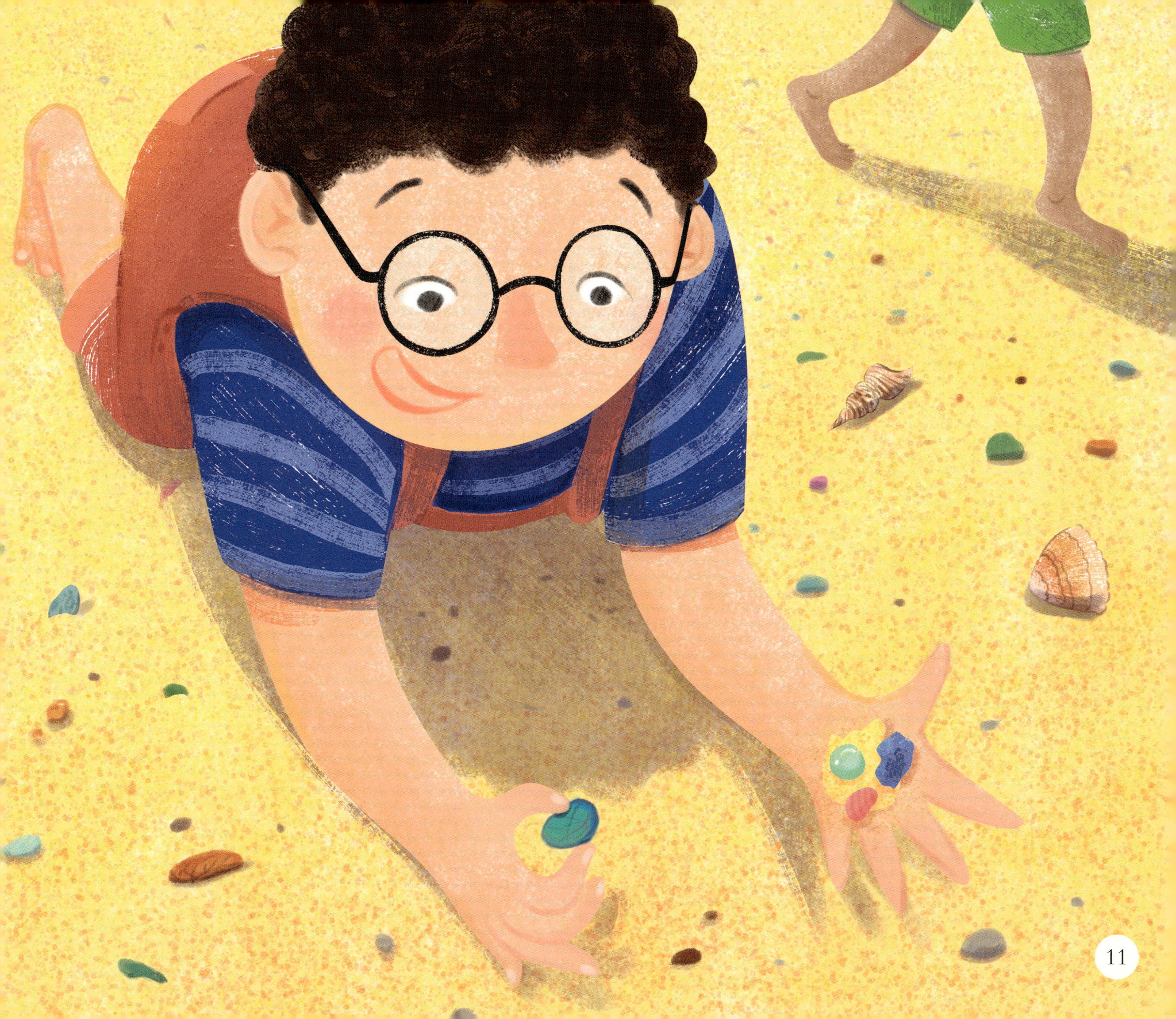

A river runs day after day,
flowing over rocks and clay.

The **riverbed** widens.
It grows deep
and forms a **canyon**
oh-so-steep.

No access while helicopter is landing or taking off

Helicopter
*** Tours ***

Blowing wind and flowing water wear down rock and carry sand.

Two of Earth's most powerful forces, wind and water shape the land.

15

The wind whips on the rocky plains, picking up clouds of sandy grains.

That **coarse** wind blows. It **scours** and scrapes, carving rocks into artful shapes.

17

Listen to the storm waves crash.
Hear the wild blue river run.

Listen to the harsh wind blow.
These are the sounds of erosion.

19

Blowing wind and flowing water wear down rock and carry sand.

Two of Earth's most powerful forces, wind and water shape the land.

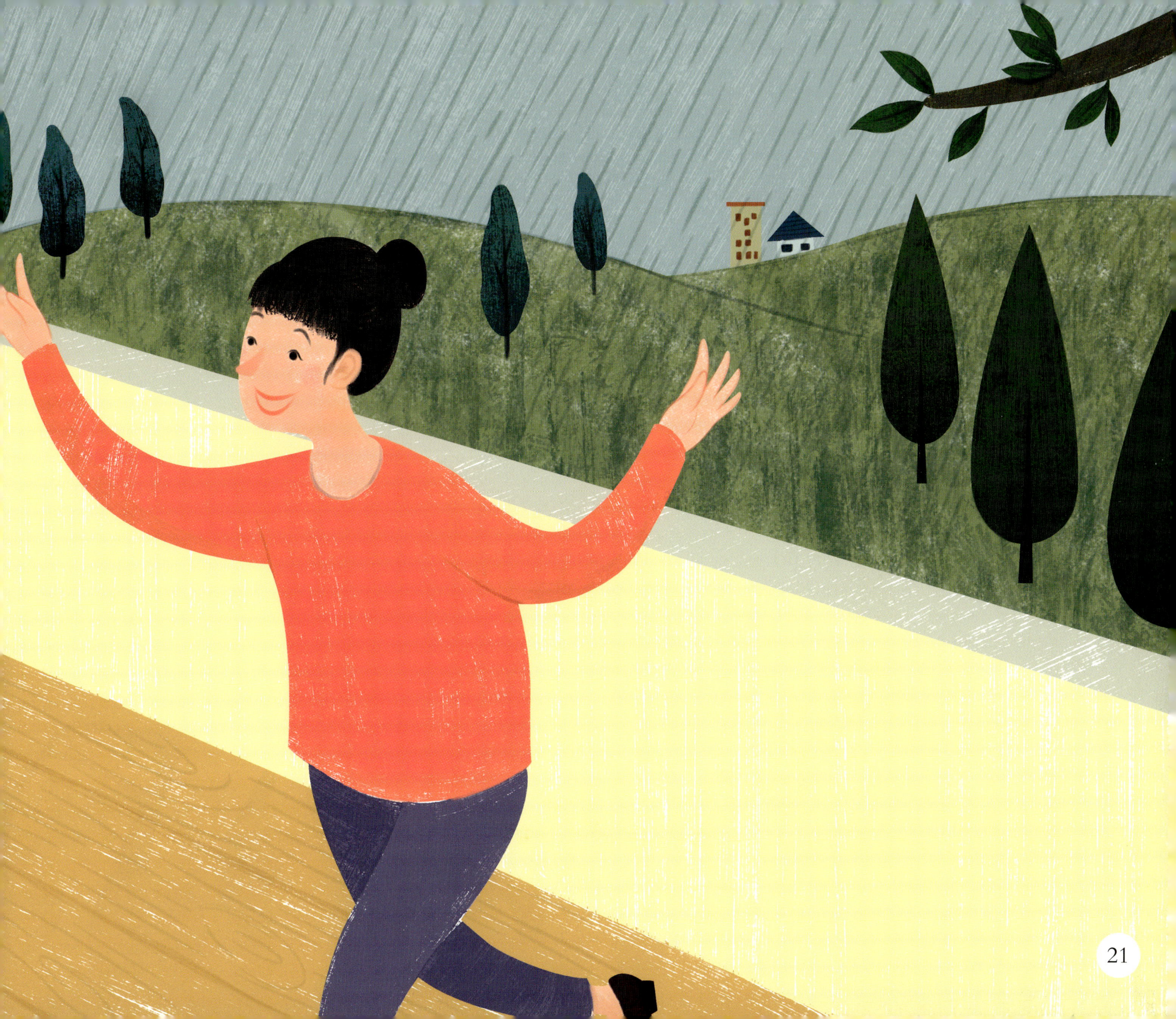

SONG LYRICS
Wind and Water Shape the Land

Blowing wind and flowing water
wear down rock and carry sand.
Two of Earth's most powerful forces,
wind and water shape the land.

With one wave, two, a million more
the ocean water pounds the shore.
Crashing waves and sprays of mist
chip away at towering cliffs.

Blowing wind and flowing water
wear down rock and carry sand.
Two of Earth's most powerful forces,
wind and water shape the land.

A river runs day after day,
flowing over rocks and clay.
The riverbed widens. It grows deep
and forms a canyon oh-so-steep.

Blowing wind and flowing water
wear down rock and carry sand.
Two of Earth's most powerful forces,
wind and water shape the land.

The wind whips on the rocky plains,
picking up clouds of sandy grains.
That coarse wind blows. It scours and scrapes,
carving rocks into artful shapes.

Listen to the storm waves crash.
Hear the wild blue river run.
Listen to the harsh wind blow.
These are the sounds of erosion.

Blowing wind and flowing water
wear down rock and carry sand.
Two of Earth's most powerful forces,
wind and water shape the land.

Wind and Water Shape the Land

Americana
Erik Koskinen

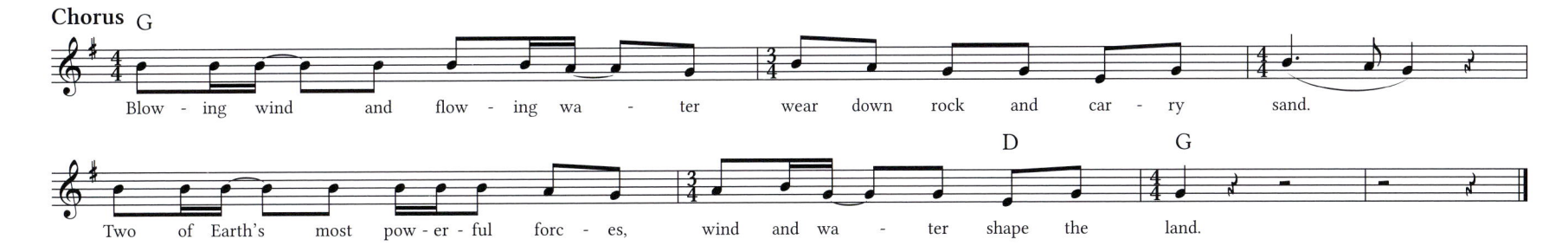

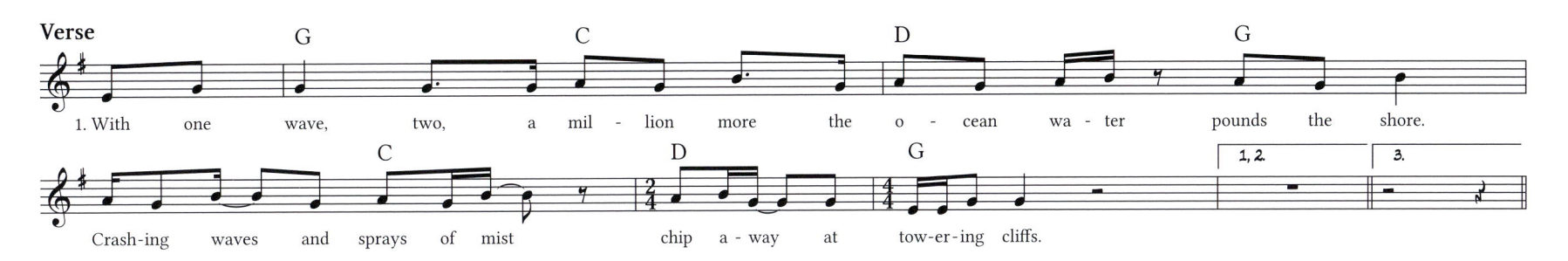

Chorus

Blow-ing wind and flow-ing wa-ter wear down rock and car-ry sand.
Two of Earth's most pow-er-ful forc-es, wind and wa-ter shape the land.

Verse

1. With one wave, two, a mil-lion more the o-cean wa-ter pounds the shore.
Crash-ing waves and sprays of mist chip a-way at tow-er-ing cliffs.

Chorus

Verse 2
A river runs day after day,
flowing over rocks and clay.
The riverbed widens. It grows deep
and forms a canyon oh-so-steep.

Chorus

Verse 3
The wind whips on the rocky plains,
picking up clouds of sandy grains.
That coarse wind blows. It scours and scrapes,
carving rocks into artful shapes.

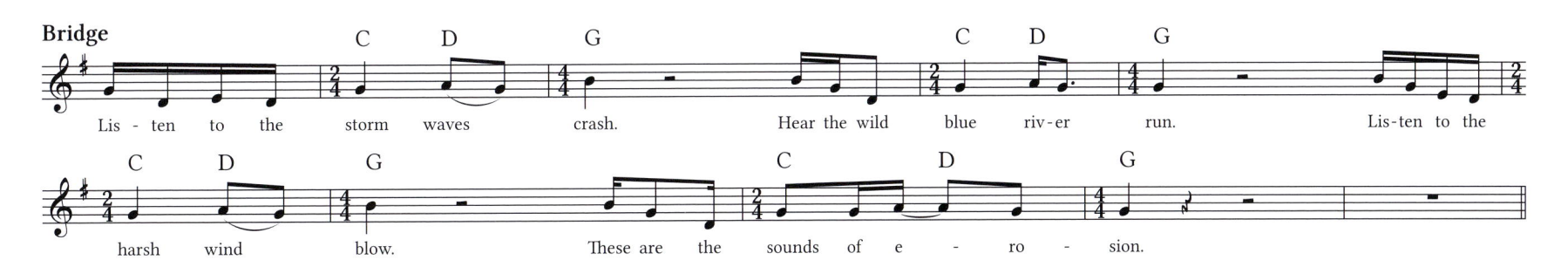

Bridge

Lis-ten to the storm waves crash. Hear the wild blue riv-er run. Lis-ten to the
harsh wind blow. These are the sounds of e-ro-sion.

Chorus

GLOSSARY

canyon—a deep, narrow valley. A canyon's walls are very steep.

coarse—rough; not smooth

erosion—how land is changed and moved by wind and water

riverbed—the land a river flows through

scour—to rub hard

GUIDED READING ACTIVITIES

1. After the next rain, go for a walk outside. Can you find signs of erosion? (Hint: Look by downspouts, streams, and puddles.) Draw a picture of what you find.

2. Try this experiment. Put a mound of dirt on a cookie sheet. That is your hill. Use a watering can to pour water on it. That is your rain. How does the rain shape the hill?

3. Listen to the song again. Every time you hear the word *wind*, wave your hands. Make your hands blow like wind. Every time you hear the word *water*, wiggle your fingers. Make your fingers fall like raindrops.

TO LEARN MORE

Dee, Willa. *Erosion and Weathering*. New York: Powerkids Press, 2014.

Rake, Jody S. *Soil, Silt, and Sand: Layers of the Underground*. North Mankato, MN: Capstone, 2016.

Riley, Joelle. *Examining Erosion*. Minneapolis: Lerner, 2013.

Salas, Laura Purdie. *A Rock Can Be*. Minneapolis: Millbrook, 2015.